The BEAUTY *and* GRACE *In* FORGIVENESS

The BEAUTY and GRACE In FORGIVENESS

Lady Fannie Mae

MILL CITY PRESS

Mill City Press, Inc.
2301 Lucien Way #415
Maitland, FL 32751
407.339.4217
www.millcitypress.net

Unless otherwise indicated, Scripture quotations taken from the King James Version (KJV)—*public domain.*

Library of Congress Control Number:

Paperback ISBN-13: 978-1-66284-747-9
Hard Cover ISBN-13: 978-1-66284-748-6
Ebook ISBN-13: 978-1-66284-749-3

TABLE OF CONTENTS

ACKNOWLEDGEMENTS

Giving honor to God, the Bishop and Shepherd of my heart. I give Him all of the glory, honor, and praise with every breath I take.

To my husband, Willie Houser.

To my blessed children. God promised to take care of them, and He did!

My daughter, N'ketia N. Spain, a former member of the Armed Forces of the United States (Navy) obtained her bachelor's degree at Phoenix University. She currently works for the Department of Agriculture as a Management and Program Analyst.

My son, Andre' D. Shaw ll obtained two degrees in clinical psychology at Florida Agricultural and Mechanical University. Andre' is the Founder of "Just An Ear Professional Listening Services".

My son, Israel L. Shaw obtained his associate of science degree in applied electronics technology. He currently works at Emory Saint Joseph's Hospital. Israel is launching his own clothing line Shaw's Enterprises, LLC.

To you, the reader. I pray that every father and mother who reads my book will choose to be better instead of bitter, and in reading this book they will find the strength and grace to forgive all of the individuals who betrayed them and caused so much pain.

"Fannie Mae Houser"

Beware of the Slander

"And forgive us our debts, as we forgive our debtors.
"Matthew 6:12 (KJV)"

Have you ever been violated to the point where God had to rescue you from yourself?

Did people of God laugh, gossip, whisper, but most of all, rejoice in your pain and overwhelming shame?

Did people watch and wait for you to lose your mind, telling you that you would turn your back on the "Bishop and Shepherd" of your entire soul, the one and only God?

Well, I have news for you. You see, my Bible tells me when you have done all you can do, *"Stand and therefore I say stand"* **Ephesians 6:13 (KJV)**. Even when you fall because you are too weak to stand all by yourself, guess what? God carries you. When you are able to stand again, He gently puts you down, and when you look back, you will see there is only one set of footprints in the sand.

"I will never leave you nor forsake you." **Hebrews 13:5 (KJV)**

When I look back over my life, I am so thankful and grateful that while I was passing through my wilderness experience, God never left me! He had a plan and purpose for my life. I had to travel through my journey of trials and tribulations in the deep dark woods. A world where all of the powers of darkness and all of the forces of hell were waiting and had set up traps, stumbling blocks, obstacles, and snares to take me out!

God was right there with me the whole time. When I didn't think I could take another step, God picked me up and carried me, whispering in my ear, *"I will never leave you nor forsake you, my child."*

This is the story of my journey through the wilderness.

It was this wilderness experience that taught me how to "Live by Faith and not by Sight".

THE BEGINNING OF A LONG JOURNEY

IT WAS THE year of 1989. My husband and I, along with our two young sons and my daughter (his stepdaughter through our marriage), were living in New York. One day, my husband said to me, "God told me to move my family to Florida." Immediately, I told him that I didn't want to move and leave my family and church. Our church was a strong foundation with a loving pastor and his wife, and was full of other young married couples, as well.

My husband and I decided we would seek God about His decision. We also agreed to speak with our pastor for clarity on whether it was God's will to relocate to Florida or not.

During one particular evening at service, my pastor called me and my husband up for prayer, along with our three children. These were the words he spoke directly to me: "Mae, the Lord told me to tell you to obey your husband as Sarah obeyed Abraham calling him 'lord'! You are to move to Florida with your husband and children. God said don't worry because everything you need will be waiting for you."

Another minister at our church told me, "God said don't worry about your daughter. She will travel the world and she will not be afraid." And the very last words the minister said to me were, "Your children will rise up and call you blessed!"

Over the next few weeks, we loaded up our U-Haul to relocate to Florida. I pondered over the words spoken to me. I didn't understand why God gave instructions only to me and did not say a word to my husband about our future in Florida.

Every word spoken was for me and my children. I wondered to myself, *Is God keeping a secret from me? Why was He so adamant about me obeying my husband and leaving everything to follow him?*

Moving and Employment

We moved in with my husband's parents when we finally arrived in Florida, although they were struggling financially. Our finances were limited, as well, because we left New York by faith with only one hundred dollars. We were blessed by the church with a truck load of food, but shortly after moving in, he gave all that we had to his mother. I couldn't believe he had given all of our finances away! We needed it for our children! I was very disturbed and unhappy because he didn't acknowledge me or consider me or our young children. This put a bad taste in my mouth and I couldn't wait to move to a place of our own.

Our sons were very young, and as long as they were with their parents, they were happy. Our daughter didn't know what to expect because she had left her family and friends. She was very nervous about her new school thankfully she met a very nice girl in her class. The middle school she attended was right down the street.

My husband was able to find a good job at Coca-Cola. We had friends who had moved from New York to Florida a few years before us. They had relatives who worked at Walt Disney World and were looking out for job openings. It was about a month later after filling out my application I was called for an interview and got a job working in the administrative department.

I was so excited to be a part of Disney World, I thought I was dreaming! I had an office job at "The Happiest Place on Earth" and I didn't have to wait a long time before becoming employed! The team I worked with in the office was kind and happy. They made me feel welcome. Having benefits and being able to provide for our children without having to depend on anyone was a great feeling.

My Disney World team was also very understanding because about three months after I started working, my younger son started having severe asthma attacks. Some days as I was driving to work, I would have to turn around and go back home to take him to the hospital. I loved my job, but our son's asthma attacks continued to get worse. My only option was to quit my job to take care of him.

Leaving my job really hurt us financially. I had good insurance, but lost it because I stopped working. Shortly afterwards, I spent most of my time having to go to the emergency room once or twice daily.

THE AFFAIR

ABOUT SIX MONTHS after we had moved to Florida, we finally found, moved, and settled into our own home. One particular afternoon when my husband was off from work, we decided to take the children to the neighborhood YMCA. Little did I know, they had built a brand new school next to the YMCA, and they had a job opening for an assistant director. I filled out the application and waited for a response at home, taking care of our son and praying for God to open doors for me to go back to work, after having to quit my job at Disney. I believe with all of my heart God had already set this new job in place just for me.

The YMCA called me the next day and offered me the job for assistance director. The job was right in the community not far from our house. Even with our youngest son having asthma, I could take him to work and give him treatments as needed. Our eldest son was going to start kindergarten in the fall and his school was about five miles from my job. Our daughter's school was less than thirty minutes away and it was a well-known high school. I had finally gotten my breakthrough and our children were settled in and happy to be in their own home!

About two years later, my world began to crumble... I found out that my husband was having an affair with one of the members from our church back home in New York. There were times I woke up during the late hours at night and heard him talking on the phone. One night, I became so curious that I woke up, grabbed the phone from my husband's hand, and asked the person, "Who are you?" The woman replied, "I am the woman who is having an affair with your man."

This was quite a blow to my ears and truly caught me off guard! I can only recall telling her, "I will not fight you in the flesh with words, but rather down on my knees." She spoke boldly and even gave me her name. My final words to her were, "You will reap what you have sown when you least expect it!"

One morning during breakfast and after my daughter had left for school, my husband made it known to our young sons that God had shown him in a vision their mother (me) being removed and

God sending him another wife. He would always wait until our daughter was out of his sight to make these comments. Can you imagine my son's precious little faces as they looked at me with tears rolling down their cheeks?

I was speechless and had to do my best to encourage my babies because they were only in kindergarten and second grade. On the way to school, I shared with them that the voice that spoke through him was not their father because their father would never say those words to them. I realized that Satan had totally taken over my husband's mind and heart!

Satan's job is to tear down the family. To kill, steal, and destroy the family by attacking the head (which is the man). Satan's plan is to disconnect the father from his children simply because the glory of a child is their father.

My husband totally turned his back on his family and stopped providing for us. On one occasion, we were all out together and he stopped by the post office, leaving us in the car. After waiting for quite a while, I decided to go inside. I walked up, stood directly beside him, and watched him send money to his girlfriend. I was speechless and he was shocked. Nevertheless, I didn't say a word.

He had stopped going to church with us and started having multiple affairs with different women. There was even a time when his stepdaughter was hanging out downtown with her friends and ran into him. When she called her dad's name, he was embarrassed in front of the lady he was with. Nevertheless, his actions broke her heart and brought her to tears.

After returning back home that evening, he told me he was leaving me because God kept showing him a vision that I was no longer his wife. I tried my best to tell him God would never tell him to leave his family, and also what he heard was not God's voice, but the voice of someone else. I asked him to talk to his parents. I also asked him if we could seek counseling from our pastor at the church.

The very next day, he spoke with his parents. They, like me, told him God would never tell a man or woman to replace their family for someone else. They also told him only Satan would speak such a lie. My husband refused to seek counseling from our pastor, and would not listen to anyone, no one could convince him that it wasn't God!

Perhaps I should have asked him why he stopped providing for his family and sent money to his girlfriend, instead. However, deep within my heart, I heard a soft voice instructing me to be still and trust God!

I believe that God is a revealer of secrets. He will always show His children what is in a person's heart and what our enemies are up to. God will repay our enemies and will go after them when we least expect it. That is why He is the revealer of mysteries. Remember in **Psalm 23:5**, God said He would prepare a table before us in the presence of our enemies.

Remember, what the enemy has planned for evil, God has a better plan for good. I have learned that we must trust God no matter what the situation looks like or how we feel inside. I was able to convince my husband that if he was going to continue with his affair, it would be best for him to move out. He agreed. I loved my husband, but I didn't want our children to believe or feel that it was okay to commit adultery.

My husband packed his things and moved into his own place. We agreed that I would bring the kids to see him on the weekends.

During those few months apart, we actually became friends again. We decided to reconcile our marriage several months later and he moved back home. Little did I know that he never stopped having his affairs. As a matter of fact, he treated me and the kids with more hostility than before.

On the weekends, when I had to go to work at the YMCA, the kids said he would lock himself up in the room and talk to *"her"* all day. He didn't bother to feed them or check on them. They were totally on their own. By the time I would get off of work, he would leave the house and go to the payphone to call *"her"* again. When the summer was over and it was time to buy all three of the children school clothes and supplies, he wouldn't contribute.

When I wasn't working, I spent most of my days and nights at the emergency room with our son who had asthma. I had visited every hospital emergency room from Sanford to Orlando Florida. I could remember spending every holiday in the emergency room.

On one occasion, our son was only three years old and had a severe asthma attack. I wanted to rush him to the emergency room, but my husband refused to take him and told me to pray. We prayed in agreement that the attack would stop, but our son only got worse, so I rushed him to the emergency room. We were told by the doctor that if we had waited a few minutes longer, our son would have died! My husband held that against me and said my job was to obey him and that it was all my fault!

Afterwards, he completely stopped paying the rent or any other bills. He would not give me anything for groceries. He stopped taking the boys to school although it was our youngest son's first year. During breakfast, he continued to remind them God was going to replace their mother and give him another wife. He would always say these things when our daughter wasn't around, she would leave early to take the school bus right across the street.

My daughter was a very bright girl in school. A good observer and listener, as well, so it was no surprise how aware she was of everything that was happening. It broke her heart because she adored her stepfather since she was six years old. He spent a lot of time with her before the boys were born. She would tell me, she never thought her parents would get a divorce, and it felt like a nightmare.

My husband had become so proud and cold; I truly believed he had a reprobate mind and was full of lust and hatred. He filed for divorce a few months later, and left us before the divorce was final.

LEFT AND ABANDONED

HOW WAS I supposed to feel after all that had happened? After being left and abandoned with a teenage daughter and two small boys? He cancelled the registration and insurance on our old car. It didn't matter that I had to get to work to provide for the family he had abandoned. It didn't matter that our five-year-old was asthmatic and needed frequent trips to the emergency room. It didn't matter if our children couldn't make it to school without a ride.

This was the man who helped raise my daughter as if she were his own. The father of our first-born son as well as our second. The three children who he had told that he loved them. Most importantly, the three children who looked up to their father each and every day! I felt helpless and afraid, and at a loss for words. I was angry! My heart was heavy, as if I were having a terrible nightmare, and couldn't wake up. Fear gripped me like a shark in the ocean.

I felt like I was in a foreign land filled with all of the forces of darkness that saw that I was all alone and afraid. There was such a deep wound inside of my heart. I didn't know the words to console my children, especially when they asked me, "Mommy, why did daddy leave us?!"

All of the life in me had gone out! I would hide in another room to hold back my tears, pretending that I was busy. I would go in the bathroom, turn the water on, and quietly scream as I fell to the floor weeping like a newborn baby. It was so hard facing my children.

I had to hide and regroup so they couldn't see me falling apart. I had to mask up with a face that said we were going to be alright. Therefore, night after night, I lay on the floor weeping and asked God to show me how to raise my babies and to please keep us safe!

I began to question myself and question God. Why did He tell me to obey my husband and leave my home, my church, and my family? Why did I have to suffer as if I had done something wrong? Why no warning? I totally didn't understand why God would allow all of this suffering and shame. I felt like Job in the

Bible: helpless, desolate, and confused. Nevertheless, there was nothing, not one thing that would keep me from looking up to heaven and calling on that great name: Jesus Christ!

Shortly after leaving us and returning back to New York, my husband called me and said his girlfriend was pregnant with his child. He asked me how I felt and said that he didn't know what to do. I recall telling him that it was a trap and snare meant to destroy our marriage. He sounded like he was confused and wanted me to tell him what to do. Suddenly, I heard someone in the background and he hung up the phone. That was the last time I heard from him until our divorce was finalized at court in Florida.

A few months later, my family told me he had married his girlfriend. I must admit that when I heard the news, I felt betrayed.

The Vow to Myself and Children

A FEW YEARS later, our son's wanted to go and stay with their dad and his wife for a while. They were still in elementary school and they had missed their dad. I made arrangements with their dad allowing the boy's to come and stay for six months. Their school records were transferred to their new school in New York. Our agreement was the boy's will return back home to Florida in the summer. After sending the boy's to their dad, weeks later I wasn't allowed to call or speak with my son's. I found out their dad whom they had missed and loved, mistreated them, making them sleep in his basement.

Our youngest son was beaten often, and they were both abused emotionally as their father threatened them not to ask to call or speak with their mother. Our sons were dressed like they were thrown away, while their children were dressed nicely. My family saw them together at the park and were shocked at the appearance of my sons. They called me and I cried when they told me. One of my relatives approached their father and told him he should be ashamed and this was not right. His new wife told my sons often that they would never have as much as their other children.

I would call and beg her to let me speak to my sons. She would just laugh and tell me "No!" before slamming the phone down in my ear. My seven-year-old wore glasses, and when he returned back home that following summer, his glasses were sent back, broken, in his case. When I went to pick up my children, I made a vow to them and to myself that I would never send them back to visit their father again unless I went with them. To this day, I have kept that vow.

As I write my story, the tears roll down my cheeks, causing me to feel the devastation of the pain all over again... but I must keep writing because this really happened. A father is supposed to love and cherish his child or children, especially a man who claims to walk with the living God.

Futile Fight for
Child Support

It was important to me to rise up early in the morning to pray and spend time with God. When the boys were in middle school, I was blessed with a better job working for Orange County Youth & Family Services. I worked for "Healthy Families Orange" as a family support worker. I was so thankful and grateful that I was able to provide a better life for my children, although it was not easy being a single mother.

I went down to the child support office, year after year, pleading for help. I called the child support office out-of-state. The out-of-state office would tell me they were waiting on Florida to comply. Florida would tell me they couldn't get through to the out-of-state office. I went down to the office on my lunch break every single chance I got because by the time I got off of work, they would be closed at 5:00 p.m.

In the meantime, their father would call and harass me early in the morning. The only reason I would answer was to let him know that I desperately needed help with the boys' clothes, school supplies, and lunches. Their needs were greater, such as sports and extra-curricular activities. My daughter had graduated from high school and joined the Navy. I would have to hang up on him because he would tell me I would never get one cent of his money. I came to the conclusion he would rather see them suffer than to provide for them. He lied and rejected all of my filing for child support.

When the child support office finally got back to me, they could never find any proof of finances in his name, and the out-of-state office said they were investigating. I was informed later that he had opened a church. Instead of getting a job and paying child support, he had opened a church and hid his assets, placing them under his wife's maiden name.

FEELINGS OF TRAUMA

WHEN THE BOYS were in high school, I received a court order petitioning me to come to court in New York. My ex had lied and said that he and his new wife had custody of our children after I had sent them to stay with them for about six months. It was impossible for him to speak the truth! He tried to do his best to keep from paying child support.

This was an insult! I was speechless and devastated by the thought of him wanting custody of our children. I feared what it would be like because he and his wife had already mistreated the boys in the past. How they hadn't even allowed them to mention my name or even ask to call me. Dressing them like they were thrown away. Telling them *"their"* children were better. Taking gifts and toys that I sent to them and giving them to *"their"* children.

I worried about my young son who wore glasses and wondered that if he should accidentally break them, would they be repaired or would "*they*" neglect him and send him back home over the summer with broken glasses again? What kind of man or woman neglects their own children?! My heart ached over and over again from the pain of my children longing for their father's love and having to accept what they couldn't change. He just didn't love them!

I was barely making it myself and trying to work to keep a roof over my children's heads. I couldn't believe he would deliberately lie about having custody of the children who he had walked out on and left for another woman. He had become a terrible father and now wanted custody of the children who I was fighting so hard to shelter and protect.

Preparing for the Trip

I STARTED PLANNING for my trip. The court order had been a random surprise, but I was ordered to attend: I had to be there. I only had a few days before leaving for New York. In this short notice, I had to inform my job and look for plane tickets, and money was short because I didn't have any extra for a trip to New York.

Being a single mother was not easy without any help from the father. I had to find someone to watch and make sure the children got to school. I had to go over the emergency plan for our asthmatic son, and pray that he didn't get sick and have an asthma attack while I was gone!

I could feel the panic washing over me. Deep inside, I felt hopeless, rejected, and alone. My heart was pounding as if it was going to explode. I did everything I could to fight back the tears. The question in my mind was always, *Why me, God?* I felt so lost for words and I thought to myself, *if I didn't have my children, I probably would give up. Lay down, escape, and run, anywhere but here.*

COURT

WHEN I GOT to court, they had a lawyer. Of course, I couldn't afford a lawyer. Having to miss a day of work really hurt my children and our finances. When I walked into the courtroom, they looked at me with eyes of hatred and pride. I must admit, I was nervous and so ashamed. I wondered, *what did I do to be hated and looked down upon so much by the man I had married and the father of our children?*

Their lawyer was so nasty and had believed all of their lies and schemes. I felt so alone, helpless, and weak. I was devastated by what I was being accused of: an unfit mother, unfaithful, and owing him child support money because he had "custody" over our children.

I was just too weak and didn't have the strength to fight all of the evil forces coming at me. I knew they were both lying about their finances because they had bought a home and had two Cadillac cars. I knew this kind of evil would take much prayer and fasting to pull down their strongholds. It appeared as if they had won the case of not having to pay me child support because he had told the judge his new wife was only a cashier and he was a preacher who had limited finances. These were all lies!

Remember, God said, *"No weapon formed against you shall prosper, and every tongue which rises against you in judgment you shall condemn"* **Isaiah 54:17 (NKJV)**. It wasn't long before they were evicted from the home they had bought. They were thrown out and lost everything, including the two Cadillac cars, and the lies about their finances and hiding the money that others gave to the church was exposed. Using people and their finances for gain and material things is wrong.

Unfortunately, many preachers like my ex live out these lies in the name of cheating families out of their money, and not paying child support to innocent children. There are some fathers right now who would rather not work than to help provide for their children. I can go on. You have already heard about other adulterous affairs. I believe they're full of lust and every kind of evil work. I truly believe those individuals have been given over to a reprobate mental state of mind. Remember, what we sow in the flesh we will also reap from the flesh!

I struggled to provide for my children and to keep them safe, teaching them the importance of forgiving their father and his wife. Although someday they would stand face to face with their father, I did not want to teach them to be bitter, but to become better than their father.

My Journey through the Wilderness

As I share my testimony, I am feeling the pain from each experience. My testimony is necessary because someone out there is hurting or will have to suffer the same way my children and I have suffered due to abandonment.

Please, hear me.

There are people in church sitting right next to you wearing a mask, smiling in your face, and waiting to rejoice when you go through the darkest times in your life. My apparently best friend rejoiced and turned her back on me until, some years later, darkness came knocking at her door. Believe it or not, I found out who my so-called real Christian friends were right in the midst of all of my darkest days, nights, and years.

It's okay when God calls us to the wilderness. Always remember that He is right there with us, sometimes even carrying us until we are strong enough to stand up to the wiles of the Devil. When we learn the wilderness, we will fight our enemies with assurance and confidence! I had to defeat the enemy of hate with forgiveness and love!

Looking back now, I know that God carried me through this tedious wilderness journey. Not only did He carry me in His arms, He gave me supernatural strength each time I fell apart. When I was too weak to go on, God picked me up and carried me. There were so many obstacles, stumbling blocks, strongholds, and, more dangerously, wolves dressed in sheep's clothing, watching, lurking, and waiting to tear me apart! But God said, *"I will never leave you nor forsake you."*

During this journey, I had two failed marriages, and when I look back, I realize it was not easy being both parents to my children. I tried to wait on God as a single mother, but I failed, thinking I needed someone to help me raise my sons because the youngest asked for a father. I realized I was doing a good job on my own, but somehow thought it wasn't good enough. I was told that there was no such thing as a super mom. A child needs a father figure, and this is true. A child does need both parents, but some adults don't want to be parents. There are some adults who cannot deal with being married to someone who has had someone else's children.

My second marriage ended when I found out later that my children were in my second husband's way. If my children were in the way and he had accepted my children when we met, what happened? I found out his plan was to send the children away to their father. This, however, was not nor would ever be my plan. My vow was to not send them away again. That was when I realized I would be fine remaining a single mom, and it was okay! I remained a single mom as I sent my daughter to the Navy after high school (it was her desire and not mine), and I sent both of my son's to college, after their high school graduation.

I know God says He won't put any more on us than we can bear. Do you recall reading earlier about the woman on the other end of the phone? Remember how I told her I was going to fight her on my knees? I want you to know that's exactly what I did. I never disrespected her or him and I never said one unkind word to them. You see, when God whispered in my ear that day in the post office, I surrendered my heart and gave everything to God.

When we surrender our all to God, no matter what darkness we face, we give up our rights and God takes total control.

God sent me on my assignment from New York to Florida and He watched over me. I had to go through the wilderness and I felt all alone. Imagine yourself in a foreign land and you are alone. You have to go through the wilderness to find your way, while all of the powers of darkness are waiting, whispering that you will never make it through the darkest years of your life! God watched over me every step of the way. Oh, yes. God was leading and guiding me through the darkness into His marvelous light. This is where I found the love of my life: my sweet, faithful Lord and Savior.

The powers of darkness had a plan for me, but so did God! Do you think I would have left New York if I had known what was going to happen? My wilderness journey made me unbreakable and unshakeable like Moses. It was a set up predestined by the "King of Kings" and the "Lord of Lords"! I had to be crushed, smashed, and squeezed in order to become the pillar of strength that I am today.

I know there are so many men and women in this world who have been through this same tedious wilderness journey. Guess what? It's your journey alone. You have been chosen. You are carrying a baby, and no one can help you until it's time to give birth. You have to learn to encourage yourself in the Lord as you get stronger. Remember **Joshua 1:9 (KJV)**, *"Be strong and of a good courage; be not afraid, neither be thou dismayed: for the Lord thy God is with thee whithersoever thou goest."* Remember, you are on an assignment!

I can laugh now because God entrusted me with this great task. God chose little old me because when I didn't know who I was, He reminded me that He had called me. When I didn't know where I was going, He said, *"I chose you to walk by faith"* I can remember God told me when someone asked me, "Who sent you?" to tell them, "I Am that I Am sent me."

I am a walking miracle. I had to learn how to trust God. When my husband left, I didn't think I could make it to see another day. I had to survive for myself and my children. We so often forget how many times we commit sin against God and others. When I look back, I can't ever remember asking God's forgiveness and not receiving it.

God sent His only Son to die on a cruel cross taking my place. I am so grateful God chose me to suffer for His "righteousness sake". I had to crucify my flesh day by day. I had to die because, one day, I knew I would have to face the people who left me and my babies for dead!

God had already predestinated a plan, setting a time in due season. Face to Face, I would look at them both not with my natural eyes, but only through the eyes of the cross, Jesus Christ.

"You intended to harm me, but God intended it for good"

Genesis 50:20 (NIV; KJV)

Forgiveness and Grace

I ALWAYS HEARD people say that the thing you fear the most will come upon you sooner or later. The Lord takes the foolish things of this world to conform the wise. About Thirteen years ago, my daughter invited her stepfather, my ex-husband, to come to her wedding because she loved him and would always be grateful for having him raise her to be a virtuous woman and good person during the ten years of her life.

As a matter of fact, she wanted him to give her away. This is what happens when you not only forgive others, but remember to teach your children to forgive, as well.

To my surprise, guess who else showed up at the wedding? His new wife. I must admit, it was a very awkward situation. I knew the day would come when we would all meet face to face; the man and woman who caused me and my children so much pain and heartache. When I first saw them, I felt nothing but anger and more anger in my flesh. I later found out we were all assigned to sit together at the same dining table. Oh, my goodness, this made me feel very uncomfortable! After we sat down, I did everything possible not to look at them for fear of painful past memories. I still didn't feel like I had been delivered from all of the hurt and pain caused by those two individuals because of what I felt.

Suddenly, there was this overwhelming feeling of acceptance and love that consumed my spirit and heart. As I turned and looked into both of their eyes, God showed me their fear and shame. I encountered a loving spirit of grace and forgiveness. Shortly afterwards, I asked them several questions about their trip and the Holy Spirit took control of my conversation. Later, during our conversation, his wife suddenly asked me to forgive her for all of the wrong they had done towards me. I uttered these words very softly, "I have waited all these years for you to ask me to forgive you because I forgave you many years ago." On that special day, we were both free!

"If the Son therefore shall make you free, ye shall be free indeed." **John 8:36 (KJV)**

So often, we think forgiveness is for someone else. True, forgiveness can set you and me free from holding a person in bondage, but most importantly, forgiveness keeps us out of the pit of bondage that bares fruits of hate, torment, illness, and unhappiness. During all of those years of pain and shame, not only was I hurting, but she was hurting, too. We often forget how many times we have sinned against God and others.

Jesus Christ shed His precious blood for me and has forgiven me over and over again. Who am I to hold an ought against my sister, brother, or anyone who has wronged me? How in the world could Jesus have ever forgiven me for all of the sins I have committed against His Word and others? He especially chose me and allowed my children's father to bring me to a foreign place where I had no family and no place to run. But instead of running back to New York when my family members asked me to come home, there was a higher power that wouldn't let me go nor look back.

Hope and Encouragement

Oh, I am so grateful God carried me through the wilderness and the fire because I would not be able to write this book and encourage you that God will never leave or forsake you. He will always take good care of you.

I write to all of the women and men who have lost husbands and wives due to an adulterous affair leaving children helpless to think it is their fault. I also write to every reader of my book because this is my greatest testimony of how God used my wilderness experience to make me strong. He gave me His grace to love those who intended to harm me, but most importantly, God taught me how to forgive those who caused me so much pain.

Some people say betrayal of a spouse is worse than having to bury a loved one because every time you see that person, you feel betrayed all over again. From my own experience, betrayal isn't pretty and will cause one to think they were responsible. Let me give you hope and encouragement. I know what you are feeling and I understand the devastation of your pain and shame. Just know, if God brought me out, he has not forgotten you.

God's Word is life and the very breath that we take every day. It will feel lonely for a while, but remember that God is taking every one of your tears and placing them in a barrow! And when you least expect it, God is going to turn all of the tears you have shed into blessings and pour them back all over you! You must stay strong. Keep praying and pouring out your heart to God!

Forgiveness is a process, so don't beat yourself up because you are hurting and it seems like the pain won't go away. Hold on to your faith in God because He's right there carrying those of you who are too weak to fight the good fight of faith. God will never abandon you! You who are struggling to find forgiveness, let God into your heart so that He can forgive through you.

I never dreamed I would be telling you my story. You have a story that others need to hear, as well. So, tie a rope and hold on to God because He is holding onto you right now as I speak!

"He that dwelleth in the secret place of the most high shall abide under the shadow of the Almighty, I will say of the Lord, he is my refuge and my fortress: my God; in him will I trust." **Psalm 91 (KJV)**

CPSIA information can be obtained
at www.ICGtesting.com
Printed in the USA
LVHW010524210622
721699LV00013B/395